# Gina Carano Fires Back

## Legal Battle Unleashed Against 'The Mandalorian' After Controversial Firing"

By

## KALL T LANE

# GINA CARANO FIRES BACK

Legal Battle Unleashed Against
'The Mandalorian' After
Controversial Firing

## Kall T Lane

# Table of contents

# INTRODUCTION

# BACKGROUND ON GINA CARANO

Gina Carano is a fitness model, actress, and former mixed martial artist who was born in the United States on April 16, 1982. As a competent Muay Thai fighter who competed in a variety of tournaments, she rose to fame in the middle of the 2000s. After a successful move into acting, Carano was able to secure roles in films such as "Haywire" (2011) and "Deadpool" (2016). Throughout her career in the entertainment sector, Carano rose to prominence as a result of her charming on-screen presence and her impressive athletic abilities.

**A Brief Synopsis of the Legal Action**:
The case that Gina Carano is involved in is around the controversial postings that she made on social media and the subsequent firing that she received from the Disney+ series "The Mandalorian." The existence of Carano on the internet became a cause of conflict as a result of posts that were judged insensitive by certain individuals, notably with relation to matters including politics,

COVID-19, and social issues. Legal steps were taken as a result of Disney's decision to cut connections with Carano, alleging infractions of corporate standards as the reason. The lawsuit highlights problems regarding the right to freedom of expression, the influence that the personal beliefs of celebrities have on their working lives, and the broader consequences for the entertainment business.

The purpose of this concise review is to lay the groundwork for a more in-depth examination of each subtopic. Please do not hesitate to get in touch with me if there are particular issues or pointers that you would like to investigate more.In this section, I will provide a concise summary of each subtopic.

The purpose of this concise review is to lay the groundwork for a more in-depth examination of each subtopic. Please do not hesitate to get in touch with me if there are particular issues or pointers that you would like to investigate more.

# CHAPTER ONE

# THE CONTROVERSIAL POSTS

**An examination of Carano's posts on several social media platforms:**

Because of the remarks that she made on social media, Gina Carano, who is most known for her part in "The Mandalorian," ignited controversy. The content of these posts included political ideas as well as statements that some people found to be insensitive. The content, the context, and the impact on Carano's public image are all aspects that are taken into consideration while conducting an analysis of her social media activity. Given the impact that celebrities wield, there are those who suggest that they ought to exercise caution when expressing opinions that are divisive. Some people believe that people have the freedom to freely express themselves, even if whatever they say is contrary to the ideas of the majority.

On a number of different platforms, Carano's posts were investigated to determine whether or not they violated any community guidelines. In light of this scrutiny, questions are raised regarding the appropriate balance between the right to free expression and the responsibility that comes with having a prominent presence online. In addition, the ever-changing dynamics of social media and the interaction of those dynamics with the personal beliefs of public people have emerged as a central topic of discussion in relation to accountability and the repercussions of actions.

## Reactions from the General Public and Opposition:

There was a wide variety of reactions from the general population in response to the contentious posts made by Carano. Fans, detractors, and impartial observers all expressed their points of view on social media sites, which turned into battlegrounds for heated arguments. The response from the general public can be broken down into several distinct categories, such as supporters who are defending Carano's ability to express herself, those who are disagreeing with her words, and those who are demanding consequences such as termination from their jobs.

Not only did the criticism expand beyond internet debates, but it also included petitions and boycotts that gained traction. The fact that audiences are increasingly holding celebrities accountable for their actions outside of the screen is reflected in this pattern. Additionally, it raises problems regarding the responsibility that firms have in controlling their public image, as well as the degree to which they should remove themselves from individuals who are the source of controversy.

Additionally, the situation sparked conversations on cancel culture, which investigated the fine line that exists between holding someone accountable for their behaviour and restricting their right to freedom of expression while doing so. On the other hand, proponents of cancel culture say that it acts as a tool for society transformation by making individuals accountable for their words and actions. Critics argue that cancel culture can sometimes be unnecessarily punishing.
the analysis of Gina Carano's social media posts, as well as the ensuing public reaction and backlash, dig into the intricate dynamics surrounding freedom of expression, accountability, and the continually developing interaction between celebrities and their followers in this age of social

media. The debates that have surrounded famous people have brought to light the importance of having an open conversation about these topics in order to promote comprehension and establish the limits of behaviour that is considered appropriate in the public domain.

# CHAPTER TWO

# THE FIRING

The term "firing" relates to the process of removing a someone from their position, and in this particular instance, we are talking about a prominent firing that is associated with Disney. There are frequently a number of elements that come into play when making judgments regarding termination, including performance difficulties, business strategy, or scandals.

**Disney's verdict is as follows**:

When Disney decides to terminate an employee, particularly a high-profile person, it is a complicated procedure that requires careful consideration of a number of different considerations. Actions taken by the individual, their public image, or their connection with the ideals of the firm could all play a role in determining this. When it comes to recognizing the broader consequences, it is essential to have a solid understanding of the reasoning behind Disney's choice.

In response, Lucasfilm has stated:
The reaction of linked businesses, such as Lucasfilm in this instance, is extremely important when a prominent figure is terminated from their position at a company. Addressing the departure, handling public relations, and maybe establishing plans for the future are all part of the process. This answer is extremely important in terms of shaping public image and ensuring that the company continues to maintain its reputation.

## Statements made to the public initially:

When it comes to constructing the narrative surrounding an incident, the earliest public statements that are made after a firing are quite important. The desire to safeguard their image, legal considerations, and transparency are all factors that are frequently taken into account when companies produce statements that have been carefully drafted. By conducting an analysis of these remarks, one can gain significant insights on the communication strategy and intents of the company.

# CHAPTER THREE

# THE STATEMENT THAT SHE MADE ON SOCIAL MEDIA

Gina Carano, who is most recognised for her performance as Cara Dune in "The Mandalorian," has been a vocal character on several social media platforms. Quite frequently, her words are reflective of her personal perspectives on a variety of subjects, including politics and social issues. Carano's attitude, which is direct and honest, has been met with both praise and criticism. She has shared her ideas on a variety of topics, including freedom of expression, individual rights, and defying cultural conventions, through her contributions on various social media platforms. When her statements are analysed, it is possible to gain insight into her worldview as well as the values that she holds dear.

**Allegations of Unjustified Termination of Employment**

Carano's exit from "The Mandalorian" created controversy, with fans and experts questioning whether or not her termination was considered to be appropriate. Certain social media posts that the actress made, which some people considered to be offensive, resulted in reaction against her. Disney, the parent business of Lucasfilm, made the decision to break connections with Carano, citing the fact that her posts contained content that was not in line with their core beliefs. As a result of the controversy that surrounded her dismissal, issues have been raised regarding the limits between personal expression and professional consequences. These questions have prompted conversations about the responsibility of corporations and the influence of social media on work careers.

**Resistance to Bullying Conducted Via the Internet**

Drawing from her personal experiences with great public attention, Carano has taken a position against abuse that occurs online. This demonstrates her dedication to making the internet a more secure place, as evidenced by her readiness to solve the problem. By relating her experiences with cyberbullying, Carano draws attention to the importance of demonstrating compassion and kindness in the realm of digital communication. Her advocacy strikes a chord III people who have experienced similar difficulties, which in turn sparks conversations about the more negative aspects of social media and the communal responsibility to cultivate an online community that is more empathetic.

It is becoming increasingly clear that Gina Carano's public statements have far-reaching ramifications, as the debates that surround her perspective continue to unfold. These statements have the potential to influence discussions on topics such as free speech, accountability, and the power relations that exist between individuals and corporations.

# CHAPTER FOUR

# LEGAL LANDSCAPE:FREEDOM OF SPEECH AND EMPLOYMENT

Freedom of speech is a fundamental right protected by many legal systems globally. However, its application in the context of employment is nuanced. While individuals have the right to express their opinions, the boundaries become critical when it comes to the workplace. Employers have the responsibility to maintain a productive and respectful work environment.

In the employment context, freedom of speech often intersects with defamation, harassment, and discrimination laws. Employees must navigate the fine line between expressing their opinions and avoiding behavior that could harm the reputation of the company or create a hostile work environment.

Employers, on the other hand, must strike a balance between respecting employees' rights and ensuring a workplace that is free from harassment and discrimination. This delicate balance is often subject to legal interpretation, and cases related to freedom of speech in employment settings have been the focus of numerous legal battles.

The entertainment industry, with its vast reach and influence, has faced unique challenges in adapting to the digital age and the rise of social media. Social media policies have become essential for entities within this industry to manage the online presence of their artists, employees, and the overall brand.

These policies typically address issues such as confidentiality, privacy, and the potential impact of online behavior on the professional image of individuals associated with the entertainment industry. They aim to strike a balance between allowing freedom of expression and maintaining a positive public image.

In the entertainment sector, controversies arising from social media posts can have significant repercussions on careers, endorsements, and public perception. Therefore, organizations often establish clear guidelines to mitigate risks and protect their interests.

Legal considerations also come into play when drafting social media policies, as laws regarding privacy, defamation, and intellectual property must be taken into account. Balancing the right to express personal opinions on social media with the need to protect the reputation of the entertainment industry is a complex task that requires careful legal navigation.

the legal landscape surrounding freedom of speech in employment and social media policies in the entertainment industry is intricate. Striking the right balance between individual rights and organizational interests is crucial, and legal frameworks continue to evolve to address the challenges posed by the dynamic nature of speech in the modern world.

# CHAPTER FIVE

# ELON MUSK'S PARTICIPATION IN THE EVENT

The engagement of Elon Musk, who is well-known for his prominent role in the world of technology and business, in supporting Gina Carano, an actress who has been the subject of controversy due to her statements on social media, has garnered a lot of attention. Musk has no problem expressing his opinions on a wide range of subjects, and he frequently makes use of social media channels such as Twitter in order to engage directly with the general public.

One of the most noteworthy instances of Musk's intervention was when he provided assistance to Gina Carano in the aftermath of her termination from a well-known television series. Musk's tweet expressing support received a lot of attention, which sparked conversations on the role that important figures have in shaping public opinion and influencing the decisions that corporations make.

The support that Musk provided for Carano also brought up problems regarding the confluence of business decisions, the impact of celebrities, and the right to free speech. Although there were those who praised Musk for his advocacy of the right of individuals to voice their thoughts, there were also those who attacked him, suggesting that his actions could be interpreted as an attempt to exert influence over the way the entertainment industry deals with contentious situations.

## The Offer That Musk Made to Support Carano

The power dynamics that exist at the junction of technology, entertainment, and free expression were brought to light by Elon Musk's public invitation to demonstrate his support for Gina Carano. In a tweet, Musk indicated that he would be interested in working with Carano on a new project. This suggests that there is a viable alternative path for individuals who are facing consequences for their opinions in established businesses.

As a result of this action, discussions have arisen over the role that digital entrepreneurs play in offering venues and possibilities for individuals who may be subject to criticism in conventional industries. In addition to this, it garnered attention to the concept of a digital domain that may provide support for a variety of opinions, even those that are considered controversial by the standards of the mainstream.

Nevertheless, the offer was subject to criticism for the possibility that it would have the effect of increasing the influence of influential individuals over public discourse. It was stated by detractors that relying on influential personalities such as Musk for support could result in the establishment of a system in which only those individuals who had access to influential backers could continue to voice their ideas without fear of retaliation.

## A Remark on the Right to Free Expression

Since Elon Musk became involved in the scandal that surrounded Gina Carano, continuing conversations regarding the right to free expression, particularly in the digital age, have been given further fuel. Musk's actions and remarks have effects that extend beyond his immediate circle, impacting conversations about the limitations of free expression. Musk is a significant person in the technology business.

Especially when it comes to individuals representing corporations or participating in industries with particular standards of behaviour, the episode provoked considerations on whether or not there are limits to the freedom of speech, and whether or not it is an absolute right. Complex problems regarding how societies negotiate the ever-changing terrain of communication are raised when personal opinions, public identities, and business affiliations collide with one another.

In addition, the role that Musk played in this scenario sparked conversations about the impact that tech moguls have on the formation of public narratives. In the current discussion regarding the role of technology in both promoting and hindering free speech, the capacity of high-profile individuals to influence opinions and influence the fate of those who are experiencing backlash for their expressions adds a layer of complexity to the discussion.
the engagement of Elon Musk in endorsing Gina Carano brought to light a variety of concerns concerning the role of influential persons in affecting conversations concerning the right to free expression. During the event, the difficulties and complexities that are inherent in striking a balance between individual expression, the expectations of corporations, and the influence of technology on the dynamics of public conversation were brought to public attention.

# CHAPTER SIX

# X CORPORATION'S ROLE

The role that X Corporation plays in the context of online platforms is multidimensional, involving a variety of areas of technology, corporate strategy, and social impact. In order to gain an understanding of the function that X Corporation plays, it is necessary to investigate its impact on digital landscapes, user interactions, and the broader ramifications for the ecology of the internet.

**The Support of X Corporation's Social Media Platforms:**

One of the most important factors that contributes to the formation of the digital landscape is the assistance that X Corporation offers to social media platforms. It is possible for this support to include the establishment of policies as well as technology infrastructure. When investigating the role that X Corporation plays in providing support for social media platforms, it is necessary to investigate partnerships, technical integrations, and the extent to which these factors influence user experiences.

The Implications of X Corporation for the Right to Free Speech on Online Platforms:

One of the most important and frequently discussed aspects is the impact that the acts of X Corporation have had on the right to free speech within internet platforms. X Corporation's rules, content moderation procedures, and involvement with issues such as misinformation and hate speech have the potential to fundamentally influence the landscape of free expression. This is because online platforms are becoming crucial locations for public conversation. In order to properly analyse these ramifications, it is necessary to investigate the equilibrium that exists between user freedom and responsible platform governance.

In light of the fact that these subjects cover a wide range of issues, I am able to provide more specific details or concentrate on particular elements if you have any preferences or special inquiries. Please tell me how you would like to continue with this!

# CHAPTER SEVEN

# THE COVERAGE OF THE MEDIA

Especially in this day and age of round-the-clock news cycles and social media, the press plays a significant part in influencing the public's impression of a situation. It is the media sources that become the key source for spreading information, forming narratives, and influencing public opinion when it comes to high-profile individuals such as Gina Carano for example.

**Responses from the Creative and Entertainment Sector**

Controversies are nothing new to the entertainment industry; nevertheless, when a prominent figure such as Gina Carano is involved, the responses from other professionals of the same profession can be rather varied. While others could choose to show their support, some people might opt to keep their distance. These responses are frequently sensationalized by the media, which contributes to the overall narrative.

Her provocative postings on social media prompted a prompt response from those working in the entertainment sector. This was the situation with Carano. It is possible for colleagues and prominent personalities in the sector to share their opinions by issuing public remarks, participating in interviews, or making use of social media. Discussions on freedom of expression, accountability, and the role of the business in addressing scandals are sparked by the multiple perspectives that are held inside the industry. These perspectives add layers to the ongoing story.

**Concerning the ongoing legal action, there is public discourse and debates.**

In the context of societal reflection, the public conversation that surrounds Gina Carano's legal activities becomes a focal point. Various channels, such as social media, online forums, and news outlets, have become arenas in which individuals engage in arguments, presenting a variety of opinions on the legal issues of the case. In order to provide the public with a more in-depth understanding, legal professionals may give insights.

Debates can include a wide range of themes, such as the limits of free speech, the influence of an individual's online profile on their professional life, and the participation of corporations in the process of responding to behavior that is deemed contentious. These discussions are amplified by the media, which provides a forum for both professionals and members of the general public to express their thoughts and participate in a more extensive conversation regarding the connection between personal expression, responsibility, and legal repercussions.

Media coverage transforms into a dynamic narrative as the legal processes go, and it changes with each new development in the case. When it comes to providing background, expert opinions, and updates on the legal procedures, the public relies on media outlets because they are hungry for information and insight.

I would like to conclude that the treatment of persons such as Gina Carano in the media not only reflects the response of the entertainment industry but also feeds public discourse on bigger societal issues. From the interconnection of the media, entertainment, and court procedures, a comprehensive narrative is formed. This narrative extends beyond the specific case at hand, delving into intricate topics such as freedom, accountability, and the ever-changing dynamics between public personalities and their viewers.

# CHAPTER EIGHT

# CARANO'S LEGAL CLAIMS

The case that Gina Carano is bringing against a specific party or parties is comprised of a number of different legal issues. It is the specifics of the litigation, including the nature of the claims, that will be determined by the information that is presented in the different legal documents. In general, lawsuits cover a wide range of issues, including but not limited to breach of contract, defamation, discrimination, and other similar infractions of the law. Due to the fact that Carano is a prominent figure, she may be negotiating a complicated legal terrain, which may involve difficulties concerning her job, reputation, or contractual duties.

**According to Carano's legal claims**:

**"Wrongful Termination"**: Carano may argue that her firing was unfair or that it violated the terms of her employment agreement or contract. - Carano may also claim that her termination was a violation of these provisions. It is possible that she will argue that the reasons that were given for her termination were not satisfactory or that the appropriate procedures were not followed.

If Carano has a contractual relationship with the party that is being sued, she may be able to assert that the other party did not fulfil its contractual obligations. This is referred to as a breach of contract. There is a possibility that this will involve breaches of particular terms, conditions, or commitments that are contained in the contract.

**Defamation**: Carano may assert that she has been the victim of false remarks or negative material that has been spread about her, which has caused her to suffer damage to both her personal and professional reputation.

-! For the purpose of proving defamation, it is typically necessary to demonstrate that the statements in question were detrimental, untrue, and made with either ignorance or malice.

**Discrimination**: Carano may incorporate claims of discrimination in her complaint if she believes that she was subjected to discriminatory treatment based on other protected qualities, such as her gender, race, or other protected characteristics.

!  Evidence of discriminatory intent and differential treatment is typically required in order to successfully pursue a discrimination claim.

**It demanded that compensatory damages be awarded.**

**Financial Losses**: Carano has the right to seek compensation for any financial losses that have occurred as a direct result of her termination, including but not limited to lost earnings, bonuses, or benefits. It is also possible that this will include future wages in the event that her termination has a significant impact on her capacity to find work that is comparable.

**Emotional hardship**: - In the event that Carano experienced emotional hardship as a consequence of the occurrences that led to the litigation, she may seek compensatory damages for the psychological impact that the case had on her. Providing evidence of the intensity of the emotional distress and its influence on the plaintiff's well-being is frequently required in order to establish emotional distress.

**Damage to Reputation**: - Those who have suffered injury to Carano's professional and personal reputation may be entitled to compensation for their losses. - It is possible that this will have a negative impact on her professional development opportunities, public reputation, and contacts within the business.

**The demand for punitive damages is as follows:**

**Malicious Conduct**: - Carano may claim punitive damages if she can demonstrate that the actions of the defendant were exceptionally flagrant, purposeful, or malicious.

-! Punitive damages are intended to both penalise the offender for their actions and discourage future behaviour that is comparable to the one that was committed.

**Deterring Others:** - The claim for punitive damages may include an emphasis on the necessity of discouraging others from engaging in improper behaviour that is comparable to the one that was committed. This provides a more general purpose for society by deterring behaviours that are seen as socially inappropriate or that are outlawed by law.

The specific evidence and arguments that are offered by both sides will determine whether or not these claims are successful in any situation that involves the legal system. A strong case must be established in court, and each claim must be backed by factual evidence and legal reasoning in order to be successful.

# CHAPTER NINE

# DISNEY AND LUCASFILM'S REACTION TO THE SITUATION

The entertainment titans Disney and Lucasfilm have, over the course of their history, encountered a variety of obstacles. The dynamics of the sector have frequently been influenced by their solutions to these difficulties. Within this section, we investigate their responses to various circumstances.

**The Management of Content That Is Controversial:**
Both Disney and Lucasfilm have been involved in content-related conflicts, which have ranged from creative choices in storytelling to decisions regarding where to cast characters. The businesses have demonstrated their dedication to addressing problems while simultaneously preserving the integrity of their artistic work. Particularly noteworthy are the conversations that have been

place on the cultural portrayal and sensitivity of their presentations.

## Taking into consideration issues of diversity and inclusion:

Over the past few years, Disney and Lucasfilm have both made efforts to improve the diversity and inclusion of their content across their respective platforms. There has been a mixture of praise and criticism directed towards the movement towards more representative narrative. The comments from the companies demonstrate a knowledge of the evolution of society as well as a willingness to fulfil the ever-changing expectations of the audience.

## Managing the Expectations of Franchise Participants:

The illustrious "Star Wars" franchise was brought under Disney's purview after the company completed its acquisition of Lucasfilm. The difficulty has been in meeting the expectations of the devoted fan base while simultaneously introducing new aspects. When it comes to the response, there is a fine balance between innovation and nostalgia, and decisions frequently cause intense debates among fans.

The fourth point is about streaming services and digital transformation:

The entry of Disney into the streaming sector, which includes the establishment of platforms such as Disney+ and Hulu, is a response to the shifting characteristics of the entertainment consumption landscape. This strategic shift is a reflection of the understanding that digital platforms are becoming increasingly influential and that there is a need to react to the changing tastes of audiences.

**Strategies for Dealing with the Pandemic:**

The entertainment sector faced difficulties that had never been seen before as a result of the COVID-19 pandemic. As a response, Disney and Lucasfilm made adjustments to their release timetables, investigated hybrid distribution arrangements, and embraced digital media for premieres. These adjustments demonstrate the companies' ability to remain resilient in the face of disturbances from the outside world.

**Due to the absence of commentary:**

Transparency and audience engagement are the first two points.

The lack of remark from Disney and Lucasfilm on particular topics can be perceived as a lack of transparency on the part of the former two companies. In a time where audiences place a high value on open communication, the decision to refrain from providing feedback may give the impression that the audience is disinterested. The cultivation of trust and comprehension can be accomplished by directly addressing concerns and actively engaging with the audience.

**The influence on the image of the brand:**
The fact that Disney and Lucasfilm have chosen not to comment on certain issues may have an effect on the company's brand image. One's silence might be construed in a number of different ways, which can result in speculation and possibly cause damage to one's reputation. When it comes to communication, taking a proactive approach is beneficial since it helps shape the narrative and maintain a positive perception among viewers.
Third, Striking a Balance Between Privacy and Transparency:

In spite of the fact that transparency is of the utmost importance, there are situations in which legal or contractual requirements may restrict comments. It can be a challenging endeavour to find a happy medium between protecting individuals' right to privacy and giving adequate information. It is necessary for Disney and Lucasfilm to handle these complications in order to resolve concerns without compromising ethical or legal norms.

## Concerning the Management of Crisis Communication:

On the other hand, a lack of commentary during times of crisis may make tensions even worse. In order to effectively communicate during a crisis, it is necessary to acknowledge the problems, demonstrate empathy, and outline the corrective activities necessary. It is necessary for Disney and Lucasfilm to devise tactics that will allow them to handle crises while minimising harm to their reputations and keeping the trust of stakeholders.

## The fifth strategy is public relations strategies:

A strategic component of public relations is commentary, or the absence of commentary to be more specific. The manner in which Disney and Lucasfilm respond to difficulties or controversies is a factor that adds to the general impression that consumers have of their respective brands. The ability to craft commentary that is both insightful and well-timed gives these organisations the ability to build narratives and positively affect public opinion.

**The following are some potential impacts on the industry:**

**1. Establishing New Standards for Studios:**
In response to issues faced by the industry, Disney and Lucasfilm have established examples for other studios to follow. The approaches that companies take, whether in the management of crises or the production of content, have an impact on how their competitors respond to situations that are comparable. Because of the ripple effects of their judgements, the norms and practices of the sector can be shaped.

**The impact on the freedom of creative expression:**
It is possible that the manner in which Disney and Lucasfilm react to scandals will have an effect on the creative freedom of producers and storytellers working within the business. It is of the utmost importance to find a middle ground between addressing issues and allowing for creative expression. It is possible that the industry will experience changes in the criteria for content development as a result of the techniques that these large companies employ.

**Third, influencing the expectations of the audience:**

There is a correlation between the responses of Disney and Lucasfilm and the formation of audience expectations. In the entertainment industry as a whole, what people anticipate from the entertainment landscape is influenced by the reactions of viewers to scandals and the subsequent acts of these organisations. In order to achieve ongoing success, it is essential to comprehend and effectively manage these expectations.

**Market Dynamics and Competition:** The impact of the industry extends to take into account market dynamics and competition. Disney's dominance in a variety of entertainment industries implies that the company's answers have an impact on the trends in the market and the strategies employed by competitors. The manner in which Disney and Lucasfilm respond to issues is closely observed by competitors, which in turn influences the decision-making processes of those competitors.

**Distribution Models That Are Constantly Changing:**

The fact that Disney has begun to embrace streaming services and digital platforms is indicative of broader upheavals in traditional distribution strategies. It is possible that the industry will continue to experience a progression in the manner in which material is distributed to viewers, with a particular emphasis on streaming and online platforms. The responses provided by Disney and Lucasfilm provide a contribution to the formation of these emergent distribution paradigms.

It may be concluded that the reactions that Disney and Lucasfilm have given to issues have far-reaching ramifications for the industry as a whole, influencing creative expression, the dynamics of the market, and the expectations of the audience. When it comes to the narrative that surrounds these entertainment titans, the delicate balance that exists between transparency and privacy, in conjunction with smart communication, plays a vital role.

# CHAPTER TEN

# PUBLIC OPINION

It is extremely important for famous people to be involved in scandals because public opinion has a significant role in defining the narrative surrounding the controversy. Over the course of the ongoing drama surrounding Gina Carano's legal actions, several conversations and responses have been generated from a variety of different quarters.

**To begin, the role of social media as an amplifier:**

Social media platforms are extremely effective at amplifying the opinions of the general people. Twitter, Facebook, and Instagram have all played a significant role in the dissemination of information regarding the issue that has surrounded Gina Carano. The trending hashtags associated with the issue are a reflection of the intensity of the discussions and the variety of viewpoints that have been expressed.

**Media coverage and editorial influence are the second factor.**

Through their coverage and commentaries, traditional media sources make a contribution to the formation of public opinion. The manner in which the debate is framed, the terminology that is utilised in headlines, and the selection of comments from essential personalities are all factors that might have an impact on how the general public views the situation. The media's ability to provide context and analysis is an essential component in the process of forming nuanced perspectives.

## Differences in Political and Ideological Perspectives:

Not only has the scandal surrounding Gina Carano sparked conversations about the activities she has taken, but it has also become entwined with bigger political and ideological conflicts around the world. In this way, public opinion is frequently divided along these lines, with individuals viewing the issue via the ideological lenses that are most important to them. The overall public discourse is being made more complicated as a result of this polarisation.

## Influencer Impact and the Relationship Between Celebrity Endorsements:

A number of influential people and public personalities, including celebrities, have expressed their opinions regarding the incident. It is possible for well-known people to influence public opinion by endorsing or condemning a certain issue. Social media platforms offer a direct route via which celebrities' points of view can be communicated to a large number of people, which means that the impact of celebrities goes beyond the realm of traditional media.

## The Development of the American Public Opinion:

Opinions held by the general public are fluid and subject to change over time in response to new information. It is possible that public mood will change as the situation develops as a result of words, acts, or the outcomes of legal proceedings. It is possible to gain a better understanding of the fluid character of society perceptions by monitoring the development of public opinion.

## A Number of Polls and Surveys Concerning the Controversy:

The first topic is methodology and representation:

There are a variety of approaches taken in polls and surveys concerning the Gina Carano scandal, which can have an impact on the accuracy and representativeness of the findings. In order to properly evaluate the data, it is essential to have a solid understanding of the demographics, sample size, and survey techniques. It is possible that online surveys, in particular, do not always reflect a cross-section of society that is representative of the whole.

## The following are the metrics for support and opposition:

Various polls are used to determine the degree of support or opposition to the activities taken by Gina Carano and the accompanying legal actions. Using these measurements, one can gain quantitative insights into the general sentiment of the target audience. It is helpful to uncover patterns and trends by doing an analysis of the variances in support across demographics.

## Variations in Regional and Cultural Expressions

As a result of regional and cultural influences, public opinion can vary dramatically from one place to another. It is possible to gain a more comprehensive knowledge of how various populations feel about the dispute by conducting polls and surveys that take into account these nuances. Some of the factors that contribute to the overall intricacy of the narrative are the differences in opinion that exist between different locations or cultural backgrounds.

## The Effects on Reputation Over the Long Distance:

It is possible that surveys will investigate the long-term effects that the incident has had on Gina Carano's reputation. The questions that pertain to her public image, job possibilities, and the perceived justice of legal actions add to a more comprehensive understanding of the consequences. When these indicators are tracked over time, it is possible to gain insights into the long-term consequences that they have on the image of a public figure.

## Analysis of the Sentiment on Social Media Sources:

Social media platforms are home to a plethora of user-generated content that accurately reflects the feelings of the general public. The techniques that are used for sentiment analysis look at linguistic patterns, feelings, and keywords in order to determine the general disposition. The combination of these digital insights with more conventional means of polling provides a multi-dimensional perspective on the attitude of the general public.

## Reactions from Fans and Requests for Change:

Emotional investment and fandom are the starting points.

It is common for fans to have a profound emotional interest in the celebrities or franchises that they support. The reactions that people have to scandals that involve persons such as Gina Carano are more than just opinions; they express a sense of loyalty, disappointment, or fury. It is vital to have an understanding of the emotional range of fan reactions in order to have a complete comprehension of the depth of their responses.
The second point is about social media campaigns and hashtags:

Through social media campaigns and hashtags, fans communicate their feelings directly to the artist. It's possible that words of support or calls for accountability will be accompanied by hashtags linked to the issue involving Gina Carano. By analysing the effectiveness of these initiatives in terms of their reach and engagement, one can gain valuable insights about the mobilisation and organisation of fan communities.

## Petitions submitted via the internet as a form of protest:

Fans frequently express their problems through the use of online petitions, in which they demand acts such as the reinstatement of certain individuals or the imposition of repercussions. Both the quantity of signatures and the demographics of those who have signed the petition can provide insight into the extent of public dissatisfaction and the manner in which it manifests itself. In addition to being symbolic acts, petitions can also be used as catalysts for change.

**The Influence on Loyalty to the Brand:**
There are implications for brand loyalty that may be derived from the reactions of fans, particularly in situations when a celebrity is associated with a specific franchise or company. It is possible for businesses to evaluate the potential influence on their audience base and the perception of the market. The opinions of fans have the potential to impact productions in the future, casting choices, and the entire image of a brand.

**Opportunities for Conversations and Interactive Participation:**
The controversy provides instances in which fans, creators, and the industry can engage in conversation with one another. The ongoing narrative is shaped by the manner in which these

interactions take place on social media platforms, online forums, and fan communities. It is possible for businesses to choose to interact with their followers in order to solve their issues or communicate their position, thereby encouraging honesty and comprehension.

the public opinion regarding Gina Carano's legal activities is complex and multifaceted. It is impacted by the dynamics of social media, the coverage of the media, polls, surveys, the reactions of fans, and online petitions. In order to gain a thorough grasp of the larger societal discourse and its ramifications for the individuals engaged as well as the industry as a whole, it is necessary to keep track of these factors.

# CHAPTER ELEVEN

# THE FUTURE OF ENTERTAINMENT

Technology breakthroughs, shifting consumer preferences, and events occurring on a global scale are all factors that are driving the transformation that the entertainment business is currently going through. When it comes to the film and television industry, Hollywood, which serves as the industry's epicentre, is suffering enormous repercussions.

**The dominance of streaming services:** How audiences take in content is being reshaped as a result of the proliferation of streaming platforms. Streaming services such as Netflix, Disney+, and others are becoming increasingly predominant, which is posing a challenge to the conventional box office models. Original content and exclusive collaborations are becoming the primary focuses of Hollywood studios as they modify their methods in order to successfully traverse this transformation.

**The importance of diversity and inclusion:** There has been an increase in the demand for narratives that are varied and inclusive. A growing number of Hollywood projects are beginning to acknowledge the significance of incorporating a diverse range of voices, cultures, and points of view. This transformation is not only in line with the changes that are occurring in society, but it also appeals to a wider audience.

( "Virtual Production:" [Reference] The production of films and television shows is undergoing revolutions as a result of technological advancements, notably in the field of virtual production techniques. Innovations in computer-generated imagery (CGI) and virtual sets are helping to boost creative output while simultaneously lowering production expenses. In an effort to maintain its competitive edge and provide immersive experiences, Hollywood is making investments in these technologies.

**"Global Collaborations," which include:** Increased collaboration between Hollywood and international markets is becoming more common. Co-productions and partnerships with filmmakers from all over the world are becoming increasingly prevalent. These partnerships and co-productions make it possible to develop stories that span multiple cultures and broaden the industry's worldwide reach.

Modifications to the Policies Regarding Social Media:

The panorama of entertainment is becoming more shaped by social media, which also plays a significant role in shaping audience perceptions and providing a platform for the marketing of content. The evolution of social media policies will have a significant impact on the future of the entertainment industry.

**Obstacles Concerning the Moderation of Content**: Platforms are struggling to adequately moderate material, which is an issue they are now facing. The conflict between the right to freedom of expression and the necessity of limiting harmful content is having an effect on the policies that govern social media. The personalities and productions of Hollywood are navigating these policies in order to communicate with audiences while remaining inside the confines of what is considered acceptable.

**An increase in the amount of interactive content:** The role of social media now extends beyond that of passive consumption. Polls, quizzes, and immersive experiences are examples of the types of interactive material that are becoming increasingly popular. These characteristics are being utilised by Hollywood in order to create interactive marketing campaigns for films and television shows, as well as to enhance fan engagement.

**Collaborations with Well-Known Influencers**: Partnerships between entertainment organisations and social media influencers are becoming increasingly common. This type of collaboration is beneficial in terms of reaching a wide variety of audience groups and generating organic awareness about upcoming releases. In the process of giving a more personal touch to promotions, influencers become an essential component of marketing strategy.

Data-driven decision making is the fourth point. The use of social media analytics is influencing the development of marketing strategies and content creation. Data insights are being utilised by publishing companies and content creators in order to gain a better understanding of consumer preferences, modify content, and improve promotional strategies. This approach, which is driven by data, is becoming increasingly important for success in the ever-changing entertainment industry.

The legal action that Gina Carano is taking against Disney

Within the realm of the entertainment sector, the legal action that Gina Carano has initiated against Disney is a noteworthy move that has brought up critical questions.

1. **The right to engage in free expression**: It is important to note that this case draws attention to the difficult balance that exists between the right of an individual to freedom of expression and the power of a firm to implement policies. Carano's termination was a direct result of the statements she made on social media, which sparked a conversation about the extent to which personal opinions should influence professionally related relationships.

**"Contractual Obligations," which include:** The provisions of Carano's contract with Disney are presumably at the centre of the legal action that is being threatened. A clause that addresses an artist's public behaviour and words is frequently included in contracts within the entertainment business. Regarding the question of whether or not Carano's termination was in accordance with the contractual obligations outlined in her agreement with Disney, the case will most certainly investigate this matter.

**The attitude of the general public and the reaction:** The lawsuit throws light on the role that the public plays in influencing the decisions that corporations make. Through the use of social media, fans and the general public are able to rapidly express their ideas, which can occasionally result in entertainment corporations taking prompt action. One is prompted to contemplate the power dynamics that exist between individuals, businesses, and public emotion as a result of the Carano case.

**An Example of Industry Standards," which includes:** When it comes to dealing with disputes that involve public statements made by its artists, the outcome of this legal lawsuit could establish precedents for how the industry handles such situations. It has the potential to impact the manner in which businesses navigate the delicate balance between safeguarding their brand image and allowing individuals to express themselves freely.

the future of entertainment will be characterised by the dynamic changes that are occurring in the landscape of Hollywood as well as the evolving role that social media will play. During the same time period, court actions such as Gina Carano's against Disney shed light on the complex link that exists between the freedom of expression, contractual duties, and the effect of public perception inside the entertainment sector.

# CHAPTER TWELVE

# CONCLUSION

**Some Thoughts Regarding the Case:**

The legal action that Gina Carano has taken against Disney is a microcosm of the wider issues that are at play within the entertainment business. In light of the case, it is necessary to consider a number of important elements that go beyond the legal actions that are currently taking place.

**The intersection between entertainment and politics are as follows**: The situation involving Carano sheds light on the growing connected nature of the entertainment and political industries. There is a direct correlation between public figures expressing their opinions on social and political problems and the subsequent scrutiny and consequences that they face. One of the issues that the entertainment business, which is frequently seen to be a reflection of cultural values, is currently facing is the challenge of tolerating varied opinions within its ranks.

On the other hand, social media can be a double-edged sword: In this particular instance, the power and effect of social media are readily apparent. Despite the fact that these platforms offer a direct conduit via which individuals can express themselves and connect with audiences, they also expose them to quick reactions from the public. The viral nature of material on social media platforms has the potential to exacerbate controversies, which can then lead to immediate consequences.

**Responsibility of Private Businesses**: Concerns regarding the responsibility of corporations are brought up by the manner in which entertainment businesses have responded to the public statements made by their performers. Studios, networks, and production corporations are coming under growing scrutiny for the way in which they handle controversies with increasing frequency. It is an issue that demands careful thinking to strike a fine balance between maintaining the image of a firm and respecting the liberties of individuals.

In terms of the impact on careers, the case of Carano highlights the potential career repercussions that can result from making public statements. Managing one's personal ideas within the context of the public realm is a challenging endeavour in this day and age, when people are intimately attached to their professional identities. When it comes to addressing these difficulties in the future, the outcome of the court action will most likely have an impact on how artists and entertainment businesses approach them.

**In the entertainment industry, More General Considerations Regarding Free Speech:**

Within the entertainment sector, the legal battle that is taking place between Gina Carano and Disney is not only about disagreements regarding contractual obligations, but it also raises broader concerns regarding the right to free speech. A deeper exploration of the complexity surrounding this matter is presented in the following points.

The Struggle to Strike a Balance Between Professional Obligations and Creative Expression: When it comes to expressing oneself personally and fulfilling their professional commitments, artists, whether they are actors, musicians, or creators, frequently find themselves in a precarious position. While the entertainment business places a high value on innovation and the contributions of a wide range of perspectives, it also places certain expectations on those who participate in it. Striking a balance that respects individual freedom without putting at risk the collaborative and brand-sensitive nature of the industry is the problem that needs to be overcome.

In this day and age of cancel culture, the following standards are constantly evolving: An further layer of complication has been introduced to concerns concerning free speech as a result of the emergence of cancel culture, which has been made possible by social media. There has been a rise in self-censorship among public people as a result of the fear of public backlash and the potential influence it could have on careers. This shift in the landscape raises issues about whether or not the entertainment business is cultivating an environment in which genuine beliefs, even if they are unpopular, can be shared without fear of severe consequences.

**The impact of corporations on the expression of ideas**: Entertainment businesses have the ability to exercise influence over the artistic expression of its artists because they are motivated by the desire to safeguard their brand image and appeal to a wide range of viewers. The extent to which a firm can restrict personal ideas outside of work is still a sensitive question, despite the fact that contractual agreements frequently describe appropriate behaviour. The difficulty of striking a fair balance that respects individual liberties while sustaining professional standards is one that calls for continual conversation and the possibility of industry-wide norms.

**The Expectations of the Public and the Responsibility to Act**: The persons who work in the entertainment sector are subject to a certain degree of duty because they are public figures. The expectations of the general public with regard to the actions and utterances of celebrities have become more intense. The difficulty lies in determining the limits of this accountability and making certain that the repercussions, in the event that they are thought required, are appropriately proportionate and equitable.

the legal action that Gina Carano has taken against Disney serves as a focus point for analysing the complexities of free expression inside the entertainment sector. In light of the case, it is worthwhile to contemplate the ever-changing dynamics that exist between personal expression, the demands of corporations, and the standards of society. As the industry continues to struggle with these difficulties, it is becoming increasingly important to adopt a nuanced strategy that protects both artistic freedom and professional duties in order to cultivate a climate that is both healthy and welcoming to creative expression.